WOMAN AND HER WISHES;

AN ESSAY:

INSCRIBED TO THE MASSACHUSETTS CONSTITUTIONAL CONVENTION.

BY

THOMAS WENTWORTH HIGGINSON,

MINISTER OF THE WORCESTER FREE CHURCH.

"Millions of throats will bawl for Civil Rights;
— *No woman named.*" TENNYSON.

BOSTON:
ROBERT F. WALLCUT, 21 CORNHILL.
1853.

To the Members of the Massachusetts Constitutional Convention:

THE publication in our newspapers of the list of members of your Honorable Body, has won the just tribute of men of all parties to the happy result of the selection. Never, it is thought, has Massachusetts witnessed a political assembly of more eminent or accomplished men. And yet there are a few to whom the daring thought has occurred,— that to convoke such ability and learning, only to decide whether our Legislatures shall be hereafter elected by towns or by districts, is somewhat like the course of Columbus in assembling the dignitaries of his nation to decide whether an egg could be best poised upon the larger or the smaller end. A question which was necessarily settled, after all, by a compromise,—as this will be.

But as, at that moment, there lay within the brain of the young Genoese a dream which, although denounced by prelates and derided by statesmen, was yet destined to add another half to the visible earth; so there is brooding in the soul of this generation, a vision of the greatest of all political discoveries, which, when accepted, will double the intellectual resources of society,—and give a new world, not to Castile and Leon only, but to Massachusetts and the human race.

And, lastly, as we owe the labor and the laurels of Columbus only to the liberal statesmanship of a woman, it is surely a noble hope, that the future Isabellas of this nation may point the way for their oppressed sisters of Europe to a suffrage truly universal, and a political freedom bounded neither by station nor by sex.

T. W. H.

WOMAN AND HER WISHES.

"EVERY book of knowledge which is known to Oosana or to Vreehaspatee, is by nature implanted in the understandings of women." This is the creed gallantly announced in that wise book of Oriental lore, the Heetopades of Veeshnoo Sarma. Probably it is from an extreme reliance on this inward illumination that we have from the same quarter of the globe the valuable suggestion — "Daughters should be made emulous of acquiring the virtues of their sex, but should be altogether forbidden to read and write." But we have changed all that, beneath our western star of empire. Those who once could not with propriety learn their letters, now have those letters conferred upon them as honorary appendages; and the maidens who once must not know A from B, may now acquire not only their A. B., but their A. M., their M. D., their F. R. S., and their A. A. S.; and are still grasping for more.

It must be confessed, however, that most of us look with distrust upon these feminine suffixes, as grammatical innovations, and are not yet prepared to go beyond the simpler combinations of the alphabet. But we all go thus far. It is a point conceded that girls shall be "educated," which is our convenient synonyme for going to school. The most conservative grant this. And the sole question now open between these and the most radical is not — Shall a woman have schooling? — but, What shall she do with her schooling when she has it?

I do not mean to say that the facilities of tuition allowed to girls as yet equal those extended to boys; but they are evidently being equalized.

As regards our Massachusetts school system, there appears to be no difference, *out of Boston*, in the opportunities given to the sexes, while the use made of those opportunities by female pupils is in most towns greater, because they have more leisure than the non-collegiate portion of the boys. Everywhere but in Boston, there is the same High School course open for the daughters as for the sons of the people. At public examinations, I have seen contests of male and female intellect, on the bloodless field of the black-board, which it tried men's souls to watch. I have seen delicate girls, whose slight fingers could scarcely grasp the huge chalk bullet with which the field was won, meet and vanquish the most staggering propositions in Conic Sections, which would (*crede experto*) scatter a Senior Class at some colleges, as if the chalk bullet were a bombshell. Let no one henceforward deny that our plans of school tuition, such as they are, have been fairly extended to girls also.

Beyond this, however, the equality has hardly reached. The colleges of Massachusetts are all masculine. The treasures and associations of Cambridge, to which so many young men have owed the impulse and enlightenment of their whole lives, are inaccessible to a woman, save as the casual courtesy of librarian or professor may give her a passing glance into Gore Hall. And it is a remarkable fact, that simultaneously with the establishment of Antioch College in Ohio, which opens an equal academical provision for women,—(under the Presidency of the father of our Massachusetts school system,)—we see in our own State the first instance of unequal educational legislation, in the proposed bill establishing male scholarships in colleges. The merits of the measure in other respects I do not disparage, but it is certainly liable to this objection. It is estimated that, even now, every graduate of Harvard has received a gratuity of about $1000, chiefly from private endowments, over and above his bills for tuition; and it is now proposed that the public shall vote, to a portion of these, $100 per annum in addition; thus still farther increasing the disproportion already created.

We are apt to felicitate ourselves, however, on the great progress achieved in female education. Perhaps we are too indiscriminate in the rejoicing. There never was a time when there were not highly educated women, according to the standard of their age.

Isis and Minerva show the value set upon feminine intellect by the ancients. We forget the noble tribute of Plato to the genius of woman, in his Banquet. We forget the long line of learned and accomplished English women, from Lady Jane Grey to Elizabeth Barrett. We forget that wonderful people, the Spanish Arabs, among whom women were public lecturers and secretaries of kings, while Christian Europe was sunk in darkness. Let me aid in rescuing from oblivion the name of Ayesha, daughter of Ahmed ben Mohammed ben Kadim, of Cordova, who was reckoned the most learned woman of her age (the tenth century) in poetry, mathematics, medicine and the other sciences which then and there flourished. In the words of the Moorish historian, "She was beautiful like a rising sun, fine and slender like a young aloe bending its head to the Southern breezes; if she ran, she looked like an antelope disappointing the sportsmen by her rapid flight; and if occupied in study or meditation, her eyes resembled the soft and melting eyes of the gazelle, looking from the top of the rock upon the burning sands of the desert. She was a well of science, a mountain of discretion, an ocean of learning." This was the Arab definition of what enlightened and chivalrous Anglo-Saxons would call facetiously a "blue-stocking," or, more seriously, "an unsexed woman."

Following the Arab practice, there were female professors of the classics and of rhetoric at Salamanca and Alcala, under Ferdinand and Isabella. At the revival of letters in Italy, the intellectual influence of Lucrezia Borgia is classed by Roscoe with that of his hero, Leo X. Vittoria Colonna and Veronica Gambara ranked as the equals and friends of Bembo and Michael Angelo; and Tiraboschi declared the Rimatrice, or female poets, of the 15th century, to be little inferior, either in number or merit, to the Rimatori, or male poets. A Pope of some eminence, Benedict XIV., bestowed on Maria Agnezi, a celebrated mathematician, the place of Apostolical Professor in the University of Bologna, in 1758. And Pope Clement XIV. (Ganganelli) wrote, in 1763, to a lady who had sent him her translation of Locke, expressing his satisfaction that the succession of learned women was still maintained in Italy.

These I cite merely as specimens of the abundant facts to be had for the asking. If I had at hand the once renowned work of Peter Paul de Ribera, entitled, "The Immortal Triumphs and

Heroic Enterprises of 845 Women," or if I had the privilege of consulting the library of Count Leopold Ferri, sold at Padua in 1847, consisting solely of the works of female authors, and amounting to 30,000 volumes, I would go more thoroughly into this branch of the subject.

I think it must, however, be conceded, on the most cursory examination, that the superiority of modern female tuition consists less in its high standard, than in its general diffusion. But when we reach this point, another serious question arises.

For it is obvious that tuition in schools is a mere preliminary to the vocation of life; and every system must be judged by its connection as a whole. Now, the great defect of our plan of schooling for girls appears to be this: that it recognizes for them no object in existence except matrimony. This will be comparatively harmless, if we assume that every woman is to be married at twenty; but as this is the experience of only a small minority, there would seem to be a deficiency in the arrangement. And in view of the probable fact, that at this moment full one-third of the women in Massachusetts are either unmarried or childless, there certainly appears to be a flaw from the outset in our educational plans.

The schooling of boys is *prospective;* what a source of mental and moral stimulus is indicated by that one word! All acquired faculties are to be brought to bear upon some definite end. The high school prepares for the academy; the academy for college; college for the professional school, perhaps; and all for some vocation where "knowledge is power." Nay, who has not seen some indolent young man, who, after wasting all the opportunities of his earlier career, was yet galvanized into industry by the professional school, because the final pressure of an immediate aim was then applied?

But what adequate aim has the tuition of girls? To fit them to be wives and mothers? But so has the boy the probable destiny of becoming a father: the father has commonly more supervision of at least the intellectual training of the children than the mother: and yet the young man has the prospect of this sacred responsibility to rouse him, and all the incentives, likewise, of professional and public duty. And if this accumulation of motives so often fails to act upon the boy, how can we expect that one alone will be sufficient for his sister?

To illustrate the manner in which this becomes apparent to an intelligent practical instructor, I quote the testimony of Mr. Smythe, of Oswego, N. Y., in a Teacher's Convention a year or more ago: —

"Mr. Smythe spoke from practical experience, having taught a large school of both girls and boys, and he had observed, that up to a certain point, their capacities or their progress was about equal. Perhaps the girls even showed more aptitude; but at that point they flagged, and there was a perceptible difference thenceforward. He had asked one young lady the reason of this, and she explained it thus: 'The boys are going into college; they have all before them; but we have nothing more to do — we are going "nowhere."' There was, he thought, an equality of talent in girls and boys; and if the former failed to evince it on any point, the failure arose from a want of stimulus. *They had no aim in society worthy to inspire them.*"

I cannot deny the truth of this. I have too often been asked, almost with tears, by young and well-taught girls, to suggest to them some employment that should fill the demands of heart and intellect; something to absorb their time and thoughts. A pupil in a School of Design once told me that in her opinion the majority of the scholars sought the occupation, not as a means of support, nor to gratify an artistic taste, but solely for the sake of an interesting employment. And in seeing the imperfect attempts to invent such employments, and the results, good in their way, but so wholly inadequate, I have almost sighed, with these discontented ones, over the one-sided benevolence of society; and felt that to give "education," without giving an object, was but to strengthen the wings of a caged bird.

Nothing can hide from me the conviction that an immortal soul needs for its sustenance something more than visiting, and gardening, and novel-reading, and a crochet-needle, and the occasional manufacture of sponge-cake. Yet what else constitutes the recognized material for the life of most "well-educated" young ladies from eighteen to twenty-five — that "life so blameless and aimless." Some, I admit, are married; some teach school, — the one miserably-underpaid occupation left open for the graduates of our high schools — the Procrustes-bed of all young female intellect. A few remarkable characters will, of course, mark out an independent path for themselves, in spite of discouragement. A few find ready for them, in the charge of younger brothers and sisters, a noble duty. A few have so strong a natural propensity for study, that they pursue it by themselves — though without any ulterior aim. Some enter mechanical occupations, which are at least useful, as employing their hands and energies, if not their intellects.

But for most of those of average energy, "to this complexion must they come at last." "It is a sad thing for me," said an accomplished female teacher, in my hearing, "to watch my fine girls after they leave school, and see the expression of intellect gradually fade out of their faces, for want of an object to employ it."

I do not claim that all young women share these dissatisfactions. They are confined to the thoughtful and the noble. The empty and the indolent find such a life satisfactory enough. "Why do you dislike to leave school?" said one young lady once, within my knowledge, to another. "Because I shall then have nothing to do," she answered. "Nothing to do!" was the astonished reply; "why, there is plenty to do; cannot you stay at home and make pretty little things to wear, as other girls do?" "But I don't care for that," pleaded the spirited and thoughtful maiden; "I don't think I was created and educated merely to make pretty little things to wear." But the protest was of no avail.

With the exclusion of women from intellectual employments, comes an accompanying exclusion from other of the more lucrative occupations, upon which I will not now dwell, "not because there is so little to be said upon it, but because there is so much." This prohibition extends even to the employments peculiarly fitted for woman, as the retail dry goods trade in our cities, which employs tens of thousands. The new Schools of Design open an admirable field for them, but one in which they already find opposition, on the ground that the introduction of female labor will create a reduction of wages in the profession; an explanation yet more discreditable to the community than the fact which it explains. In Lowell, the average wages of women are estimated at $2.00 per week, (deducting board); those of men at $4.80, for toils not longer, and often no more difficult. In some of our towns, female grammar-school teachers are paid $175 per annum,—and male teachers $500, for schools of the same grade, and of smaller size. The haunts of sin and shame in our great cities can tell some of the results of these criminal irregularities.

But the question of employments, important though it be, is still a secondary one. Indeed, it will ultimately settle itself. It is not apparent that *men* have anything to do with it, except to secure fair play, which is less difficult here than in some other matters. Energetic women will make their way into the avocations suited to them, and the barrier once broken down, others will follow. *La carrière ouverte aux talens*, is the only motto. No one can anticipate the results, and it is useless to dogmatize. "Let them be sea-captains if they will," said Margaret Fuller, speaking only perhaps in some vague memory of readings in Herodotus, and of the deeds of Artemisia at Salamis; but soon after, the newspapers were celebrating the name and fame of Miss Betsey Miller, captain for these dozen years of the Scotch brig Cleotus. Yet woman, it would appear, is "constitutionally disqualified for action." It would be pleasant to see the grave author of this phrase on board Capt. Betsey's brig, beating into the port of Belfast in a gale of wind. It is to be feared, however, that he would be constitutionally disqualified for remaining above the hatches.

The test of sphere is success. If Miss Miller can walk the quarter-deck; if Madame Grange can argue cases in court; if Mrs. W—— can conduct the complex business transactions of a great Paris house; if Maria Mitchell can discover comets, and Harriet Hosmer carve statues; if Appolonia Jagiello can fight in one European revolution, and Mrs. Putnam vindicate another (besides having the gift of tongues); if Harriet Hunt can really cure diseases, and Lucretia Mott and Antoinette Brown can preach good sermons, and Mrs. Swisshelm and Mrs. Nichols edit successful newspapers; then all these are points gained forever, and the case is settled so far. Nor can any one of these be set aside as an exceptional case, until it is shown that it is not, on the other hand, a *test case;* each person being a possible specimen of a large class who would, with a little less discouragement, have done the same things.

That there are great discouragements, it is useless and ungenerous to deny. For every obstacle that a man of genius is admired for surmounting, a woman surmounts an hundred. If any one of the aforesaid women has attained to her position without actual resistance or ridicule, then *that* is the exception, for these things are the rule. Margaret Fuller's biographers did not stoop to tell the whole story of the petty insults and annoyances which she incurred, in the simple effort to take the place which belonged to her. Some critics have doubted the propriety of Elizabeth Barrett's venturing to write such vigorous verses; woman should be "the lovely subject of poetry," these gallant gentlemen think, not its author; they do not, however, contract for the production of the article from their own brains of a quality equivalent to the "Drama of Exile." Even *Punch* considers female physicians to be fair game; as if the wonder were not, that any delicate woman should employ any different attendance.

The first lesson usually impressed upon a girl is, that the object of her instruction is to make her more pleasing and ornamental; but of her brother's, to make him more wise and useful. Parents, pulpit and pedagogue commonly teach her the same gospel. If she opens book or newspaper, she finds the same theory. I forget from what feeble journal I cut the following:—"A sensible lady writes us as follows: 'Woman's true mission, about which so much has been written, is to make herself as charming and bewitching as possible to the gentlemen.'" Yet what is this but Milton's "He for God only, she for God in him"? We have but to turn to the books nearest at hand for abundant illustrations of the same thing.

"Women ought not to interfere in history," says an eminent writer, "for history demands action, and for action they are constitutionally disqualified!" Shades of Queen Bess and Margaret of Anjou, of the Countess of Derby, Flora McDonald, and Grace Darling!

"This difficult statement requires some qualification," says another, "if the reader be young, inexperienced, *or a female.*"

Goethe said that "Dilettanti, and *especially women*, have but weak ideas of poetry."

It seems hardly credible that even Dr. Channing, in an essay "on Exclusion and Denunciation in Religion," should have reflected quite severely on "women forgetting the tenderness of their sex, and arguing on theology." For if, as a recent Convention preacher declared, "Among the redeemed, up to this time, an immense majority are women," one would suppose that their experimental knowledge of religious matters might partially counterbalance a trifling deficiency in the Hebrew tongue—which is not, indeed, a quite universal accomplishment among the male sex.

It is strange to see that when men try to rise highest in their advice to women, they so seldom rise beyond this thought, that the position of woman is but secondary and relative. An eminent Boston teacher, who has done much for female education, astonished me when I read, in the "School and Schoolmaster," his unequal appeals for the school boy and school girl: —

"That boy on yonder bench may be a Washington or a Marshall. * * * * That fair-haired girl may be [what? — not a Guion or a Roland, an Edgeworth or a Somerville? — no, but] the future *mother* of a Washington or a Marshall! By inspiring her heart with the highest principles, you may do much to advance humanity, by forming a sublime specimen of a just *man*." And so on.

I have heard the indignation expressed by young women on occasions like this; once, especially, after a Normal School examination, when this had been the burden of the addresses of the excellent gentlemen there present. "They all spoke," said the indignant girls, "as if the whole aim of a woman's existence was to be married, and we all wished that we might never be married, so as to prove that there were other noble duties in life for us, as well as for young men. They would not have spoken so to *them*."

Now, with this immense difference, that precisely where the stimulus is applied to young men, there the pressure of discouragement is laid on girls, it cannot be expected that the faculties of the latter for different employments should be developed with equal ease. The varied functions suitable to women will be filled more slowly, for the same reason that it takes twice as long to ascend the Ohio against the current, as to descend by its aid. But it has well been asked, "If woman's mind be really so feeble, why is she left to struggle alone with all those difficulties which are so sedulously removed from the path of man?"

There is, moreover, this inconvenience, that although greater strength may in certain cases be developed by this encounter with prejudice, it is apt likewise to mar the symmetry and grace of the character; and hence the occasional charge of unfeminine unattractiveness against distinguished women. Mill, with his usual penetration, enumerates among common fallacies, the impression, that because one extraordinary member of a class is rendered conceited or offensive by the isolation, the whole class, if elevated, would show the same qualities. Make education and station accessible to all women, and the source of annoyance will disappear.

I repeat, however, that even the question of employments is a secondary one. The avocations of many men are as little stimulating to the intellectual nature as those of women. Comparatively few men are educated by their employments. The great educator of American men is the ballot-box, with its accompaniments.

By its accompaniments, I mean the whole world of public life, public measures, public interest and public office. From direct participation in this school of instruction, the American woman is not only more rigidly excluded than the woman of any other Christian nation, but this takes place under circumstances of peculiar aggravation, precisely because more importance is attributed to this sphere among the Americans than elsewhere. It is a startling fact, that in the land where the right of political action is most universal, most prized, and most jealously guarded *among men*, it should be most scrupulously denied to women. In most European countries, the sexes stand nearly on a level in this respect; the distinction is not of sex, but of station. A few men can be kings, peers and prime ministers—a few women can be queens, regents and peeresses. The masses of both sexes are equally far removed from direct participation in public affairs, and hence woman, *as woman*, is neither degraded nor defrauded.

Indeed, some of the most eminent European statesmen and thinkers of the last century have argued against the principle of universal suffrage, on the ground that it must, if consistently established, include women also. This was the case, for instance, with Pitt and Coleridge. Talleyrand said, "To see one half of the human race excluded by the other half from all participation in government, is a political phenomenon, which, on abstract principles, it is impossible to explain." "The principle of an aristocracy is admitted, (says De Tocqueville,) the moment we reject an absolutely universal suffrage."

On the other hand, among English democrats,—as Godwin, Bentham, and the authors of the People's Charter,—there is the same ready recognition of the abstract right of woman to this prerogative.

And yet, in the United States, in which alone the experiment of Democracy is claimed to have been tried;—here, where all our institutions must stand or fall by their conformity to the abstract idea of equality;—here, where, moreover, (says De Tocqueville again,) "politics are existence, and exclusion from politics seems like exclusion from existence";—here, one half the race is still excluded. Tennyson sums it all up in his "Princess"—

> "Millions of throats will bawl for Civil Rights;
> —*No woman named!*"

Not to name her is, in a Democratic government, to ignore her existence; and hence, one cannot be surprised to read, in one of the ablest commentaries on American institutions, the cool general remark, "In the Free States, except criminals and paupers, *there is no class of persons* who do not exercise the elective franchise." Women are not even a "class of persons;" they are fairly dropped from the human race: and very naturally, since we have grown accustomed to recognize an "*universal* suffrage" which does not include them.

It is no wonder that, under these circumstances, we Americans are remarkably polite to women. It will take a good many bows and delicate homages to atone for this unexpected result of free institutions,—leaving one-half the population with less access to political power than they have under monarchies. With an awkward impulse of compensation, we attempt to atone for our fraud by courtesies. We rob woman of her right to the soil she stands upon, and then beg leave to offer her a chair. "Chivalry," said the brilliant German woman Rahel, "was a poetical *lie*, necessary to restore the equality of the sexes." Is our American chivalry of the same stamp?

The most fascinating of modern Catholic writers, Digby, brings it as a charge against republican institutions, that they are "in the highest degree inimical to the influence and importance of women." And one can hardly deny their tendency to fix more permanently that withdrawal of rights and substitution of favors, which has always been the ground of complaint among intelligent women. It is singular, too, that in a country where the customary standard of female schools is higher than any where else, the opportunity of females for public service should be less than in most of the nations of Europe.

In England, "in a reported case, it is stated by counsel, and substantially assented to by the Court, that a woman is capable of serving in almost all the offices of the kingdom; such as those of Queen, Marshal, Grand Chamberlain, and Constable of England, the Champion of England, Commissioner of Sewers, Governor of a Workhouse, Sexton, [parish clerk,] Keeper of the Prison, of the Gate House of the Dean and Chapter of Westminster, Returning Officer for Members of Parliament, and Constable, the latter of which is in some respects judicial. The office of Jailor is frequently exercised by a woman."

In an action at law, it has been determined that an unmarried woman, having a freehold, might vote for Members of Parliament; and it is recorded that Lady Packington returned two. The office of Grand Chamberlain, in 1822, was filled by two women; and that of the clerk of the crown, in the Court of Queen's Bench, has been granted to a female.

At the coronation of King Richard II., Dame Margaret Dimock, wife of Sir John Dimock, came into court and "claimed the place to be the king's champion, by the virtue of the tenure of her manor of Scrinelby, in Lincolnshire, to challenge and defy all such as opposed the king's right to the crown." The Countess of Pembroke, Dorset and Montgomery, had the office of hereditary sheriff of Westmoreland, and exercised it in person. At the assizes at Appleby, she sat with the judges on the bench.

In the reign of Henry VIII., when, during some family quarrels, Maurice Berkely and others entered the park of Lady Anne Berkely, at Yate, and committed depredations, the lady complained to the king, who immediately granted her a special commission under the great seal, to inquire into the matter. She then returned to Gloucester, opened the commission, sat on the bench in the public Sessions Hall, impanelled a jury, received evidence, and finally sentenced the rioters.

A statement has passed current, originating with Gilbert Stuart, to the effect that the Anglo-Saxon Queens were accustomed to assist at the Parliaments convoked by their husbands. But I have not been able to find confirmation of this in the authorities to which he refers — William of Malmesbury and the Anglo-Saxon Chronicle. It is not improbable, however, in view of the fact that during that period, a prioress might preside over a meeting of ecclesiastics, and legislate for the government of the church; and might take precedence in rank in the assembly, as was the case in the Council of Becanceld, convoked in the year 694.

It is a remarkable fact, that one of the most important treaties of modern Europe—the peace of Cambray, in 1529—was negotiated by two women—Margaret, the aunt of Charles V., and Louisa, mother of Francis I.

It is strange to turn from such a wide variety of public stations to the very different provisions of our own nation, which is yet so much more liberal of office to its male population. "In the United States," says Judge Hurlbut, "a woman may administer upon the estate of her deceased husband, and she has occasionally held a subordinate place in the Post Office Department. She has, therefore, a sort of post-mortem and post-mistress notoriety; but with the exception of handling letters administrative and letters mailed, she is the submissive creature of the old common law." This would seem rather an inadequate result, for woman, of American Revolution, Declaration of Independence and Constitution; and even suggests doubtful comparisons with the days when "the Great Squaw Sachem" ruled the inhabitants of Eastern Massachusetts, from Mystic to Agawam.

It would seem that under the circumstances, the rising protest of American women, though it may annoy men, can hardly surprise them. I have chosen to begin with the consideration of education, because that is a point commonly conceded, and therefore a good fulcrum for the lever. But much more remains behind. It is not the sole grievance of woman that she has not even her full share of school-education.

Nor is the complaint only, that any system of "education" is utterly imperfect which provides for women only schools, and not functions.

Nor is it the whole of the grievance, that the employments easily accessible to women are few, unintellectual and underpaid.

Nor is it all, that the denial of equal political rights being an absolute wrong, must necessarily be in many ways a practical wrong. Is not each individual, male or female, an unit before God? Has not woman, equally with man, an individual body to be protected, and an individual soul to be saved? Must she not see, feel, know, speak, think, act for herself, and not through another? We hear much said of the value of the "franchise of a freeman," say women. But why should Franchise belong to Francis more than to Frances, when the three words are etymologically the same, and should be practically so; all signifying simply, Freedom? Nay, as things now stand, Frank may grow up a vulgar, ignorant ruffian, and Fanny may have the mental calibre and culture of Margaret Fuller or Mary Lowell Putnam, — the self-devoted energy of Dorothea Dix or Mary Ware: yet it will make no difference. The man must count as one in the State, the woman counts zero; a ratio, as mathematicians agree, of *infinite* inferiority.

But this is not all. Nor is it all that this exclusion is a thing done without "the consent of the governed." "The body politic (says the Massachusetts Constitution) is formed by a voluntary association of individuals." Accordingly, we think it a daring responsibility to hold a Constitutional Convention, or even to pass a Liquor Law, without a popular vote thereon. When was the popular vote taken, in which women relinquished even the rights conceded to them by their English ancestors? At any given moment, there is probably a clear majority of women over men in this commonwealth. Have this majority consented to their present subjection? No, they have had no opportunity to consent; they have never been asked; they have only *acquiesced*, as the black majority in South Carolina acquiesce, because that very subjection has made them both ignorant and timid.

Nor is it all, that we lose the services of the purest half of the human race from our public offices. Not one of these admirable women, whom I have just named, may have a direct voice in legislating for a hospital or a prison; not one of these accomplished ones can have a place in even a school-committee; to say nothing of those grander cares of state, which were yet freely granted to Elizabeth of England and to Maria Theresa.

Nor is it all, that female labor thus loses its guarantee of protection, which political economy has always recognized as an important feature of free institutions. "To give energy to industrial enterprise," says one American writer, unconscious of the covert satire, "the dignity of labor should be sustained; the franchise of a freeman should be granted to the humblest laborer who has not forfeited his right by crime. In the responsibilities of a freeman, he will find the strongest motives to exertion. Besides, so far as government can by its action affect his confidence of a just remuneration for his toil, he feels that a remedy is put in his hands by the ballot-box." Indeed, John Neal asserts that the right of suffrage is worth fifty cents a day, in its effect upon the wages of male laborers, in this country.—But where are all these encouragements for women?

Nor is it all, that with the right to labor, all the other rights of woman, as to person and property, are equally endangered by this exclusion from direct power.

For the great grievance alleged by all women who make complaint of grievances is this: that all these details are but part of a *system*, which lies at the basis of all our organizations, assumes at the outset the inferiority of woman, merges every married woman in her husband, and imposes upon every single woman the injustice of taxation without representation;—symbolic of the general fact, that she incurs most of the responsibilities of freedom, without its rights.

"Husband and wife (says Blackstone) are held to be one person in law, so that the very being and existence of the woman is suspended during the coverture, or entirely merged and incorporated in that of the husband."

Nor is this to be an empty claim. "The husband has the right (says another legal authority) of imposing such corporeal restraints as he may deem necessary for securing to himself the fulfilment of the obligations imposed on the wife. He may, in the plenitude of his power, adopt every act of physical coercion which does not endanger the life or health of the wife."

"In short, (says Judge Hurlbut,) a woman is courted and wedded as an angel, and yet denied the dignity of a rational and moral being ever after."

The protest of women, therefore, is not against a special abuse, but against a whole system of injustice; and the peculiar importance of political suffrage to woman is only because it seems to be the most available point to begin with. Once recognize the political equality of the sexes, and all the questions of legal, social, educational and professional equality will soon settle themselves.

It is not to be denied, that the subject is coming rapidly into discussion, and bids fair to be ably handled. On the one side are the reports of three large and estimable "Woman's Rights Conventions," in Worcester and Syracuse, together with a series of ten tracts, by the same indefatigable band of agitators. On the other side are the fixed observances of Church and State; nearly every stripling editor in the land has winged his goosequill in defence of established institutions; reverend divines have quoted Scripture, and grave professors quoted Aristophanes; and nothing has been left undone, except to reprint old John Knox's tract of A. D. 1553, entitled, "Blast of a Trumpet against the Monstrous Regiment of Women."

It is an unfortunate thing for this last party, that every one of their arguments is vitiated by the fact, that it has been used heretofore in defence of every oligarchy and every slavery. The rebellious females are assured, first, that they do not really wish for any farther political rights; second, that they do not need them; third, that they are not fit for them. To which the fair malcontents reply — like malcontents in all ages, fair or foul — first, that they know what they wish; second, that they know what they need; third, that they know what they are fit for, and intend to secure it.

I. Upon the first point, I can only here say, that men have, as men, nothing to do with it. This essay is entitled "Woman and her Wishes," because I conceive that to be, *for men*, the main point at issue. The final choice must be made by women themselves. The final question must be, What does woman, after all, desire? It may be still as difficult to ascertain this as in the days of the wandering knight, in the old English legend; but it is essential. I do not understand, however, that any man is called upon to settle this question. We are not to interfere, except to secure fair play. I have not heard that the most ardent apostles have proposed to compel any woman to make stump-speeches against her will; or march a fainting sisterhood to the polls, under a police in Bloomer costume. Let there only be fair play. The highest demand of each; that is her destiny. "Let them be sea-captains *if they will*," and that is all.

II. Upon the second point, that women do not *need* additional civil rights, there is more to be said.

I do not understand it to be asserted by any one, that women have no influence, because they have no direct political power. Margaret Fuller is right on this point; "it needs only that she be a good cook, or a good scold, to secure her *influence*, if that were all." There never was a time when she had not this, however totally the theory of society may have excluded her. Demosthenes confessed that "measures which the statesman has meditated a whole year, may be overturned in a day by a woman." The shrewd Ganganelli (Pope Clement XIV.) said well that "many women who appeared only as the wives of princes or ambassadors, and who are not even mentioned in history, have frequently been the cause of the grandest exploits. Their counsels have prevailed, and the husbands have had all the honor due to the sagacity of their wives." And Montesquieu complains of those who "judge of a government by the men at the head of affairs, and not also by the women who sway those men." "*Soignez les femmes*," Napoleon used to say to his emissaries; "Secure the women!"

It is upon a different ground that the complaint proceeds. "Woman should not merely have a share in the power of man — for of that omnipotent Nature will not suffer her to be defrauded — but it should be a *chartered* power, too fully recognized to be abused." "It is always best (remarks another advocate) to add open responsibility, where there must at any rate be concealed power."

The question lies here. Woman must have influence somehow: shall she have it simply, directly, openly, responsibly? — or, on the other hand, by coaxings, caresses, dimples, dinners, fawnings, frownings, frettings, and lectures after the manner of Mrs. Caudle? It is possibly true, as Miss Bremer's heroine says, that a woman may obtain any thing she wishes of her husband, by always keeping something nice to pop into his mouth; but it is quite questionable whether such a relation can rank any higher in the scale of creation, than the loves of Nutcracker and Sugar Dolly in the German tale.

Besides, there is this fatal difficulty, that woman, with all her powers of domestic coaxing and coercion, has never yet coaxed or coerced her partner into doing her simple justice. Shall we never get beyond the absurd theory that every woman is legally and politically represented by her husband, and hence has an adequate guarantee? The answer is, that she has been so represented ever since representation began; and the result appears to be, that among the Anglo-Saxon race generally, the entire system of laws in regard to woman is at this moment so utterly wrong, that Lord Brougham is reported to have declared it useless to attempt to amend it; "there must be a total reconstruction, before a woman can have any justice."

The wrong lies not so much in any special statute, as in the fundamental theory of the law. Yet no candid man can read the statutes on this subject, of the most enlightened nation, without admitting that they were obviously made by *man*, — not with a view to woman's interest, but to his own. Our Massachusetts laws may not be so bad as the law repealed in Vermont in 1850, which *confiscated to the State* one half the property of every childless widow, unless the husband had other heirs. But they must compel from every generous person the admission, that neither justice nor gallantry has yet availed to procure any thing like impartiality in the legal provisions for the two sexes. With what decent show of justice, then, can man, thus dishonored, claim a continuance of this suicidal confidence?

There is something respectable in the frank barbarism of the old Russian nuptial consecration, "Here, wolf, take thy lamb." But we cannot easily extend the same charity to the civilized wolf of England and America, clad in the sheep's clothing of a volume of Revised Statutes; — caressing the person of the bride, and devouring her property.

For I believe that our laws do give some protection to the person, and that our courts would hardly sustain the opinion of the English Justice Buller, that the husband might lawfully "correct" his wife with a stick not larger than his thumb — "so great a favorite is the female sex of the laws of England," as Blackstone says. Yet if he should do so, I see but an imperfect remedy. For no woman's cause had ever a trial by a jury of her peers; she may not even have half the jury composed of such as herself, though this privilege is given to foreigners under the English laws. And the wrongs of the outraged wife, or the bereaved mother, can only be adjudged by a masculine tribunal.

It was thought very ludicrous when the female petitioners in

New York craved permission to address the Assembly in person, instead of leaving their cause to men. But I apprehend that if that change were made here, the spectacle would not again be seen of a bill to protect the property of married women being refused a third reading, by a large majority, in the Massachusetts House of Representatives, "after a considerable discussion, *mostly of a humorous description.*"

"The perfection of woman's character (said Coleridge) is to be characterless. Every man would like to have an Ophelia or a Desdemona for a wife." This last proposition is perhaps too universal a statement; yet grant it, and the sad question still recurs, "But what was the *fate* of Ophelia and Desdemona?"

III. To the third suggestion, that woman is not *fitted* for any additional political rights, there is much to be said; and yet little that has not been said by others.

1. For instance, it can hardly be seriously urged that women are not qualified to vote intelligently, since the direct and irresistible protest of the address of the petitioners to the Massachusetts Constitutional Convention: —

"It would be a disgrace to our schools and civil institutions, to argue that a Massachusetts woman, who has enjoyed the full benefit of all their culture, is not as competent to form an opinion on civil matters, as the illiterate foreigner, landed but a few years before upon our shores, unable to read or write, not free from early prejudices, and little acquainted with our institutions. Yet such *men* are allowed to vote."

2. Another argument is met as explicitly by a resolution of the first Woman's Rights Convention in Worcester: —

Resolved, That it is as absurd to deny all women their civil rights, because the cares of household and family take up all the time of some, as it would be to exclude the whole male sex from Congress, because some men are sailors or soldiers in active service, or merchants, whose business requires all their attention and energies.

3. It is said that women are not now familiar with political affairs. Certainly they are not, for they have no stimulus to be. Give them the same motive for informing themselves, and the natural American appetite for newspapers will be developed as readily in women as in men.

4. There is fear of undue publicity. "Place woman, unbonneted and unshawled, before the public gaze, (wrote the exquisite critic of the New York Christian Inquirer,) and what becomes of her modesty, her virtue?" But surely, the question of publicity is already settled, to the utmost extent. At least, every man must be silent who acquiesces in the concert, the drama, or the opera. I will not dwell on the exposures of the stage, or the indelicacies of the ballet. But if Jenny Lind was "an angel of purity and benevolence," for consenting to stand, chanting and enchanting, before three thousand excited admirers; if Madame Sontag could give a full-dress rehearsal (which does not commonly imply a superfluity of costume) for the special edification of the clergy of Boston, and be rewarded with duplicate Bibles; it is really hard to see why a humble woman in a Quaker dress — yes, or any other — may not bear her testimony against sin, before as large an audience as can be assembled to hear her.

"Oh, but," men say, "it seems different, somehow, to hear a Quaker woman speak in public!" Yes, but *is* it different? Are right and reason to depend on the color of a dress? It has been said that "a saint in crape is twice a saint in lawn." But why is a drab-colored Amazon more tolerable than any other?

We repress a woman's tongue in public, and then complain that she uses it disproportionately in private. But if she has any thing worth saying in the one case, why not in the other? Surely, there is no want of physical power. Jenny Lind can fill as large a concert-room as Lablache. Nay, there is another aspect to the argument. Often, at conventions of men, amid the roughness and the gruffness of tone, the stammering and the hesitating, when I have recalled to memory the clear, delicious voice of Lucy Stone, "gentle and low, an excellent thing in woman," yet penetrating with its quiet fascination to the utmost corners of the largest hall — never loud to the nearest, never faint to the farthest, and bearing on its quiet current all pure womanly thoughts and noble aspirations — I have almost wondered at the tolerance of Paul in suffering a *man* to speak in public.

And let those who, even after this, cling to the idle thought that such a public career is incompatible with the more modest graces, (which are becoming, not to feminine character only, but to human character,) — let such persons read the stainless record of Elizabeth Fry's inner life, in the most intoxicating periods of her noble career: —

"It was indeed an act of faith," says her journal, in describing a public address; "I have a feeling of unfitness and unworthiness for these services more than I can express. On entering the assembly, I hardly dared look up; when I did, I thought there must be fifteen hundred persons present; but I may, I think, say it was, before I ended, a glorious time; the power of the good spirit appeared to reign over us."

5. But the great anxiety, after all, seems to be for the dinner. Men insist, like the German Jean Paul, on having a wife who shall cook them something good. I confess to some sympathy with these. I, too, wish to save the dinner. Yet it seems more important, after all, to save the soul. It is a significant fact, that several female authors, as Mrs. Child and Miss Leslie, have had to *work their passage* into literature, by compiling cookery-books first; just as Miss Martineau thinks it well to vindicate Mrs. Somerville's right to use the telescope, by proving that she has an eye to the tea-table also. Let us consent to this, and only supplicate, that after the cookery-book is written, and the table set, the soul of the woman may be considered as free. Let us value the dinner, for it is well that labor should have its material basis, as life has; but let us remember that a woman who provides for that, and that only, is, after all, but a half-woman, of whom Mrs. Jellyby is the other half.

It is to be admitted, however, that among the "domestic virtues" there are functions nobler than the culinary department. Yet how strange the blindness that hopes to educate these by crushing all other faculties. And how strange a narrowness of estimate is often left, even after this blindness is partially removed. For instance, some critic said, after speaking very cordially of Mrs. Mill's able article on "the Enfranchisement of Woman," in the Westminster Review, that "it was to be hoped, however, that the mother of J. S. Mill would always regard it as her chief honor to have reared her distinguished son." But, in the name of common sense, why so? Is it not as much to *be* an useful woman as to rear an useful man? Why postpone the honor from generation to generation? or when will it be overtaken? Or, rather, what incompatibility between parental and social duties? The father may be as important in the rearing of the child as the mother; (indeed, Jean Paul says, with exquisite truthfulness, that the mother marks the commas and semicolons in the son's life, but the father the colons and periods;) yet it is not considered the whole duty of man to be a good father. John Adams contrived to train John Quincy Adams, and to be a parent and guardian of American liberty likewise; why should woman content herself with one half the mission?

And there are facts enough to vindicate my position. Victoria is at the head of a kingdom and of a household,—and neither of them a small one; and she fulfils both vocations well. The most eminent of American Quakers stated it to me as the general experience of this body, that the female members most publicly useful, are also the best wives and mothers. Certainly, the twenty-five grandchildren of Elizabeth Fry rose up to call her blessed, none the less, because she was the valued adviser of all the leading British statesmen, and the guest or correspondent of half the sovereigns of Europe. Nay, it is touching to read, that in the very height of her public labors, "Mrs. Fry's maternal experience led her to give some advice about the babies' dress, (at the Paris Enfans Trouvés,) that it might afford them more liberty of movement."

6. In the disorder now sometimes exhibited at our caucuses and town-meetings, there is plainly an argument, not for the exclusion, but for the admission of women. They have been excluded quite too long. Observe the different character of public dinners since their admission there, which yet would have seemed as unpardonable to our grandfathers. Such is my faith in the moral power of woman, that I fear we cannot spare her from these scenes of temptation. There was wisdom in that hearty recognition given by a party of rough California miners to some brave New England women who were crossing the Isthmus, in the rainy season, to join their husbands. "Three cheers (said they) for the ladies who *have come to make us better!*"

We need the feminine element in our public affairs to make us better. I cannot agree with those who deny that there are certain differences of temperament between the sexes; God has a great purpose in these; let us not deny them, nor let us waste them. It is precisely these feminine attributes which we need in all the spheres of life. Wherever the experiment has been tried (as among the Quakers) it has proved successful: it will yet be tried farther. The noble influence of Manuelita Rosas, in Paraguay, over the policy of the stern dictator, her father, is but a hint of what is yet to come, when such influences shall be openly legitimated. Woman, as a class, may be deceived, but not wholly depraved; society may impair her sense, but not her self-devotion. Her foot has been cramped in China, and her head every where; but her heart is uncramped. We need in our politics and in our society a little more heart. The temperance movement would lie dormant in many of our towns, but for the sympathies and energies of women. The anti-slavery movement had hardly made its way to the masses till a woman undertook to explain it. And the Western editor's objection to the "Woman's Rights movement" seems to me to be one of its strong points; that "if it should prevail, we may yet see some Mrs. Stowe in the Presidential chair."

It sounds strange to American ears to hear of a woman as head of a nation. But our English ancestors, three centuries ago, living under the government of a woman, would have been equally astonished to hear of a commoner as being at the head of a nation. Any innovation seems daring until it is made, and when once made, it is called "an institution," and then any farther change is daring.

The fatal inconsistency of those who protest against any innovation in the position of woman, lies in the fact that they have tolerated so many innovations already. Once admit that she has been wronged, and the question then recurs, whether she has yet been fully righted. We have conceded too much to refuse farther concessions. She must be a slave or an equal; there is no middle ground. If it is plainly reasonable that the two sexes shall study together in the same high school, then it cannot be hopelessly ridiculous that they should study together in college also. If it is common sense to make a woman deputy postmaster, then it cannot be the climax of absurdity to make her postmaster general, or even the higher officer who is the postmaster's master. Methinks I hear again the old shout of the nobles at Prague, "*Moriemur pro rege nostro—Harriet Beecher!*"

Is it feared lest there be a confusion in the nature of the two sexes, from these wild propositions? But nature commonly provides adequate means in seeking an end. If those distinctions are not strong enough to protect themselves, it is useless to try to guard them. Lucy Stone said, "woman's nature is stamped and sealed by the Creator, and there is no danger of her unsexing herself, while His eye watches her." Nature has every thing to dread from constraint, nothing from liberty. The only demand of our female reformers is to be set free. Beyond that, let all decisions be made by those whose business it is. "Woman and her Wishes" is the title of this essay, not woman controlled by the wishes of man. As the powers of the body are divided between the sexes, (physicians say,) giving man the greater power of exertion, and woman the greater power of endurance, so it can hardly be doubted that a shading of difference, without inferiority, runs through all the spiritual natures of women and of men. Of these let there be an union such as God joins and man cannot put asunder; an equal union of hearts, of homes, of lives, of rights, of powers; not tyranny on the one side, disguised as courtesy, — nor criminal self-extinction on the other side, where God demands only a noble and mutual self-consecration.

"Then reign the world's great bridals, chaste and calm,
Then springs the crowning race of human kind."

www.ingramcontent.com/pod-product-compliance
Lightning Source LLC
LaVergne TN
LVHW011142110826
845150LV00008B/2471
9781418192730